My mother is a lady who has had a lot of problems in her life. Most of them me....

DIANA BRISCOE

Sometimes she pretends not
to see me, when I behave very badly.

CAMILLE FRASER, AGE 8

If I aggravate my brother
she sends me to bed without any food.
I keep on thinking I won't
do it again, but I keep on doing it.

MORAG, AGE 8

My mother is very patient.
She would have to be
with five kids,
four dogs and two jobs.

PAM REPEC, AGE 12

Mom defies the logic of time,
beats the rules of time and
space travel 'cos she can be wherever
she is needed,
whenever she is needed.

STUART & LINDA MACFARLANE

What Every Mother Deserves

A huge bouquet
of flowers.

Specially made
designer outfits.

Diamonds, sapphires
and other
precious stones.

To live in the
Garden of Eden.

The greatest child
in the world.

What a Mother Gets

A wilting
dandelion.

A daily pile
of dirty laundry.

Pebbles from
the beach.

A garden to
weed and tend.

Me – well one
out of five isn't bad.

STUART & LINDA
MACFARLANE

The Love Instinct

Moms can take care
of midnight coughing fits,
nosebleeds, nightmares
and the dire effects of
too many unripe apples,
while still
not fully conscious.

PAM BROWN, B.1928

Moms have a unique ability to cope when things go wrong for their children such as when they fail exams or fall off a bike. On these occasions a million worries run through her head, a thousand scenarios play out within her mind – yet while all this is going on she smiles reassuringly and calmly says, "Don't worry – everything's going to be all right."

BRIAN MCLEAN

A DOCTOR CAN HEAL,
A NURSE CAN BANDAGE
BUT ONLY A MOM
CAN KISS AWAY
THE PAIN.

STUART & LINDA
MACFARLANE

A mother is a woman with a twenty~five hour day who can still find an hour to play with her family.

IRIS PECK

She pretends to be cross
– but then just spoils me rotten.

HELEN THOMSON

A mother stands No Nonsense.
Well – not much.

PAM BROWN, B.1928

MOTHER'S DAY 4AM

A mother is the lady who looks
surprised and delighted
when her children bring
her breakfast at four o'clock
on Mother's Day.

PAM BROWN, B.1928

Mother's Day is the one day in the
year when she shouldn't have to do the
housework, the washing, the ironing,
the dishes.
On this very special occasion all these
tasks should be completely
forgotten – the only trouble is that she has
to catch up on the work the next day.

STUART & LINDA MACFARLANE

Any mother
could perform the
jobs of several
air traffic controllers
with ease.

LISA ALTHER, B.1944

All mothers are physically
handicapped.
They have only two hands.

AUTHOR UNKNOWN

Since time immemorial
mothers have been able to do
at least six things at the same time.

PAM BROWN, B.1928

The law of motherhood states that someone will need mom desperately as soon as she sits down.

MAUREEN VALENTINE,
FROM "HIGHLINE NEWS" SEATTLE

Why do all families call out: "Maaaaam, the cat's been sick!"

PAM BROWN, B.1928

Everyone wants to save the earth. No one wants to help Mom dry the dishes.

P. J. O'ROURKE

It is in the Bible re Sunday: you must not work, nor thy son, nor thy daughter, nor thy manservant, nor thy maidservant, nor thy cattle, nor thy stranger that is within thy gates. Poor Mom.

PETER CAREY, FROM "THEFT: A LOVE STORY"

FACTS: Each and every day a woman will do twelve times as much housework as her husband and thirty times as much as her children. But who's counting?

STUART & LINDA MACFARLANE

There are supreme tests
of endurance. Climbing Everest.
Crossing the Gobi.
Sailing single-handed round
the world.
Being a mom.

PAM BROWN, B.1928

One hour with a child is
like a ten-mile run.

JOAN BENOIT SAMUELSON,
FROM "NEW YORK TIMES"

Mothers are obliged to develop
elephant hides, to resist the glares of the
childless, when a normally
sober-minded child runs berserk, or throws
potato chips on the café floor,
or goes completely rigid
to resist being put into its buggy.
And screams. And screams.
Perhaps heaven will be revenged – and send
them six or seven of their own.

PAM BROWN, B.1928

MOMS ~ TEA POWERED

Cars need petrol –
mothers need tea.

STUART & LINDA MACFARLANE

WORRY! WORRY! WORRY!

Dear Mother: I'm all right.
Stop worrying about me.

EGYPTIAN PAPYRUS LETTER

Mothers sit every exam,
play every match,
perform every part.
And end up more exhausted
than the children.

PAM BROWN, B.1928

Mothers face emergencies
wonderfully well.
They have rehearsed them all.

PAMELA DUGDALE

I used to be a reasonably careless and
adventurous person before I had
children: now I am morbidly
obsessed by seat-belts
and constantly afraid that
low-flying aircraft will drop on
my children's school.

MARGARET DRABBLE, B.1939

Babies!

It is not advisable to put
your head around your child's door
to see if it is asleep. It was.

FAITH HINES

Women can hear higher
frequencies than men.
This means it's much easier for
them to hear the sound
of a baby crying.

STUART & LINDA MACFARLANE

A baby's bowels are triggered
by starting the car engine,
buttoning the last button on
her very best white dress, welcoming
a sophisticated friend –
or simply boarding the aircraft.

PAM BROWN, B.1928

If a baby is going to disgrace
you it will only be on an occasion
of extreme embarrassment.

PETER GRAY

Besotted New Mothers

Long before speech,
a baby has learned that Charm Pays.

PAM BROWN, B.1928

Dear mothers, gazing with love at
the babies in their arms.
Let them not realize for a little while
that these small smiling creatures
will grow to be teenagers.

PAMELA DUGDALE

A tiny, new, baby daughter is a giant
phone bill waiting to happen.

STUART & LINDA MACFARLANE

[Motherhood is] calling a doctor to a child with a temperature of 104 degrees who is sitting up smiling by the time the doctor arrives, and not calling a doctor for fear of incurring his wrath while the child's appendix bursts.

KATHARINE WHITEHORN, B.1928,
FROM "ONLY ON SUNDAYS"

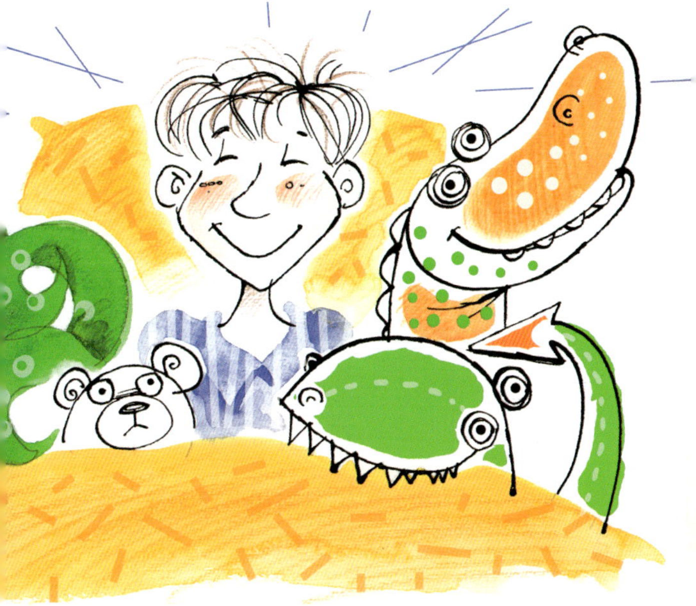

A MOM IS SUPPOSED TO LOVE YOU AND WASH BOYS' SMELLY SOCKS

SALLY ARTHY

The best thing I thought she did
was having me, but
others might not think so.

TIM TRIPP, AGE 12

I wouldn't swap my mother
for the world
– a new bike maybe – but not the world.

STUART & LINDA MACFARLANE

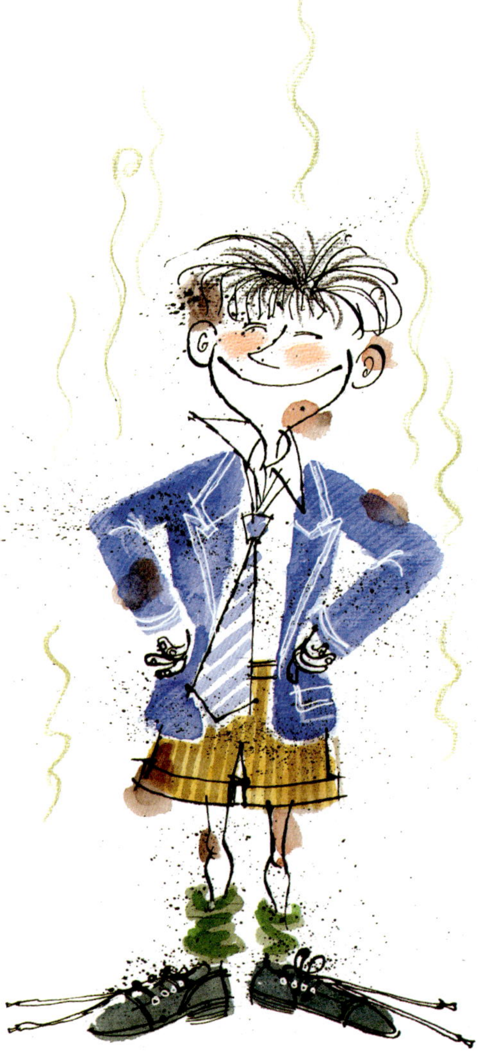

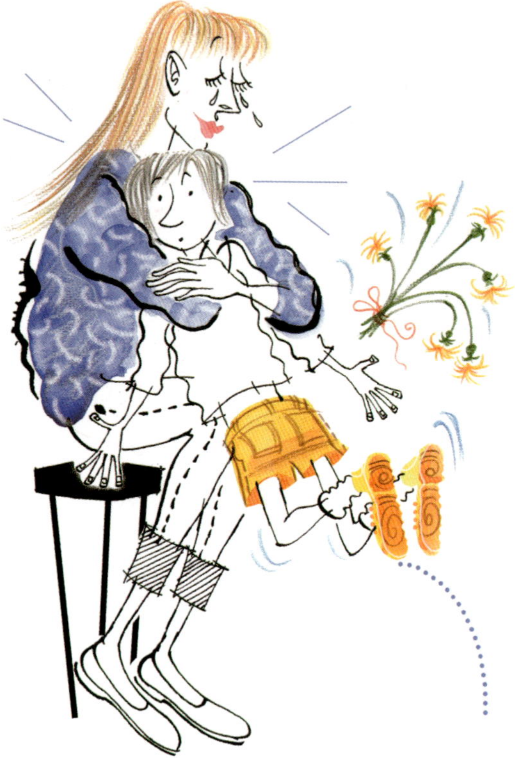

Silly Moo!

She is a person who cries
when you do something bad,
and cries even harder
when you do
something good.

ROBIN DIBIASE, AGE 14

A mother is a female parent.
Somebody to make the beds and wash up.
Someone to wake you too
early and make you go to bed too early,
and some one to see that you *always*
do your piano practice.

SUSAN, AGE 11

Mothers are vultures that hang over
you, telling you that you have to
clear the snow or make your bed.
They nag at you, giving you lectures
on life in general and how
to make your bed in particular.

PETER, AGE 12

A mom is someone who always asks you to do something when you're just about to do something else.

GENEVIEVE, AGE 12

There's a part
of every man which
resents the great bossy
woman that once
made him eat up his
spinach and
wash behind his ears.

KATHARINE WHITEHORN, B.1928

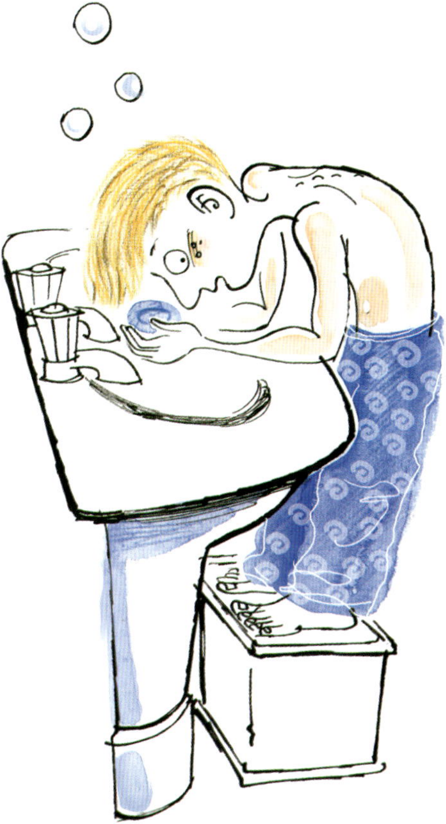

Mommys are nice except when they find gum sticking to their carpet.

MICHELLE, AGE 10

She sometimes gets mad
and once she got so mad that she made
us make our own Breakfast.

MARK, AGE 9

I sometimes think that they are
bossy and bad tempered but when I think
about it I realise how hard it is
to be a mom. It is make breakfast, wash up,
go shopping, cook dinner, wash up,
put feet up, collect the kids from school.
I can see why they ask you
to wash up or get your own tea.
I begin to wonder why they ever become
mothers in the first place.

ALAN, AGE 15

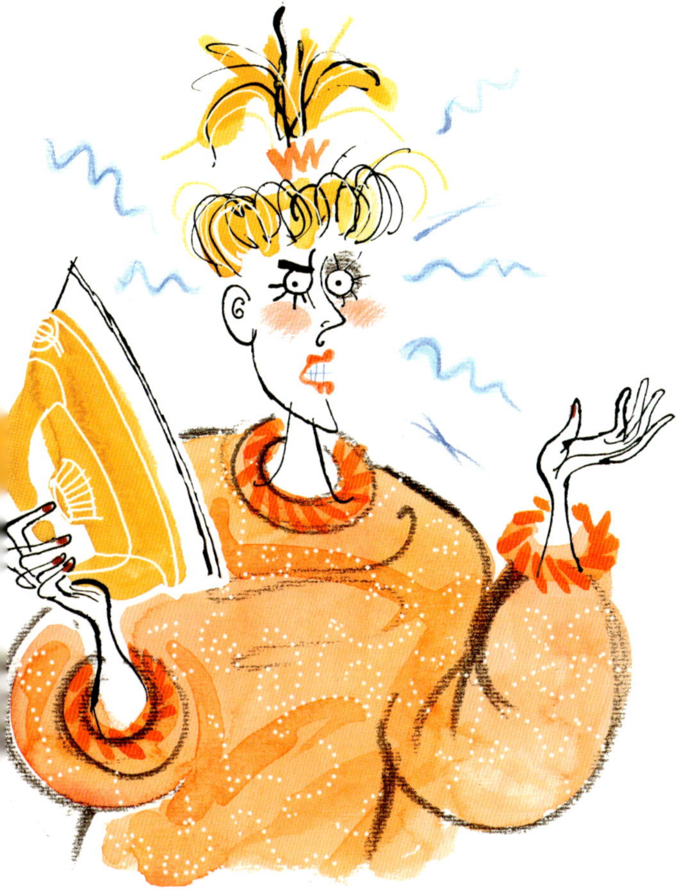

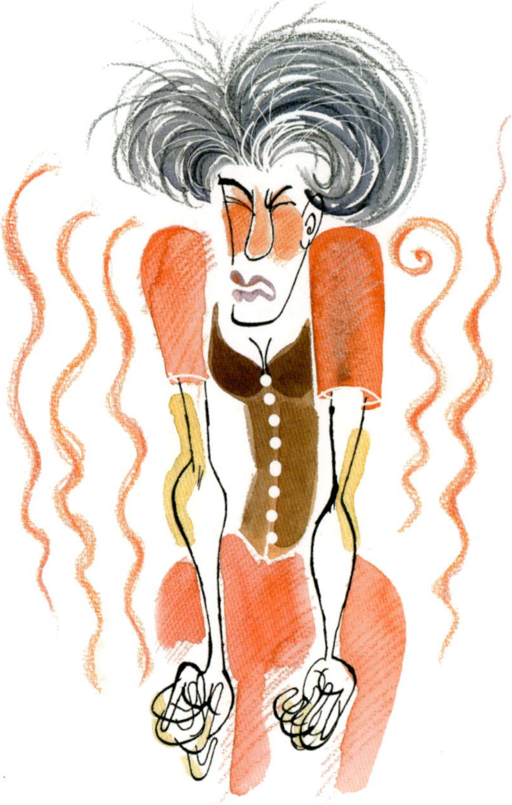

Mothers are people who sit up worrying about you. When you come home they holler at you.

GARY CREES, AGE 13

Mothers are like volcanoes
about muddy puddles on the floor.
Like prehistoric monsters.
Like cars screaching
on a wet morning.
When the door bell goes,
– the telephone rings,
– the baby cries.
Some mothers get in a rage,
rushing all over the place.
My mother does.

PHILIP, AGE 7

WORKING MOTHERS

There is no such thing as a
NON-working mother.

HESTER MUNDIS

My mommy teaches managers
and she does the washing for me.

BEN TIDY

At work, you think of the children
you have left at home. At home, you
think of the work you've left unfinished.
Such a struggle is unleashed
within yourself. Your heart is rent.

GOLDA MEIR (1898–1978)

It is very difficult to write a great
novel, a Definitive Work,
when you are trying to out-think kids
twenty-four hours a day.

PAM BROWN, B.1928

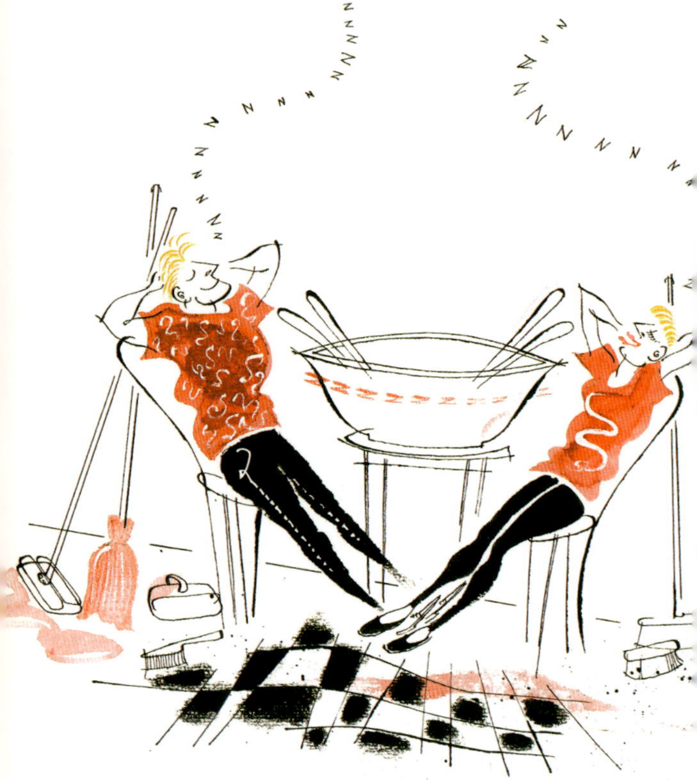

How many
kids does it take to
change a light bulb? None
— Mom will do it.

STUART & LINDA MACFARLANE

Women never have
an half-hour in all their lives
(excepting before or
after anybody is up in the house)
that they can call their own,
without fear of offending or of
hurting someone.

FLORENCE NIGHTINGALE (1820–1910)

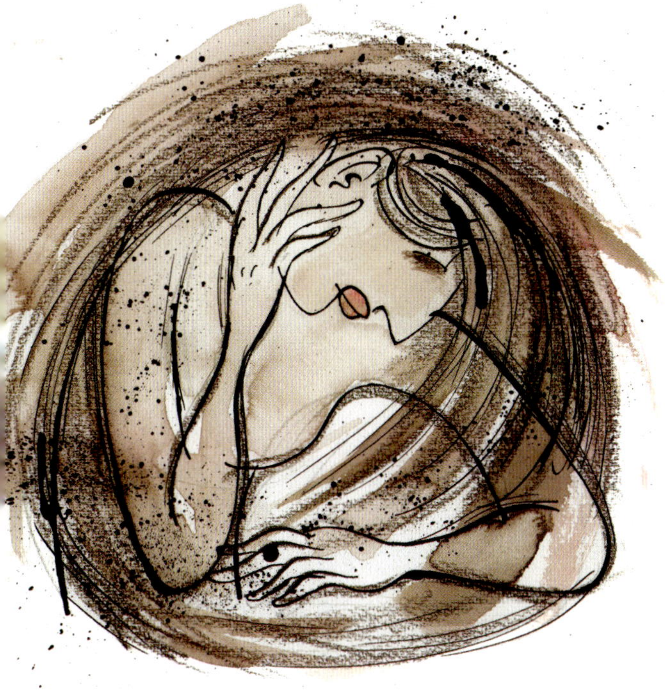

No matter how old a mother is, she watches her middle-aged children for signs of improvement.

FLORIDA SCOTT MAXWELL (1883~1978)

Mothers have every intention of letting you go, letting you lead your own life, never interfering. But they just can't help phoning to see if you have enough socks. And are eating properly.

PAM BROWN, B.1928

I blame Rousseau, myself. "Man is born free", indeed. Man is not born free, he is born attached to his mother by a cord and is not capable of looking after himself for at least seven years (seventy in some cases).

KATHARINE WHITEHORN, B.1928

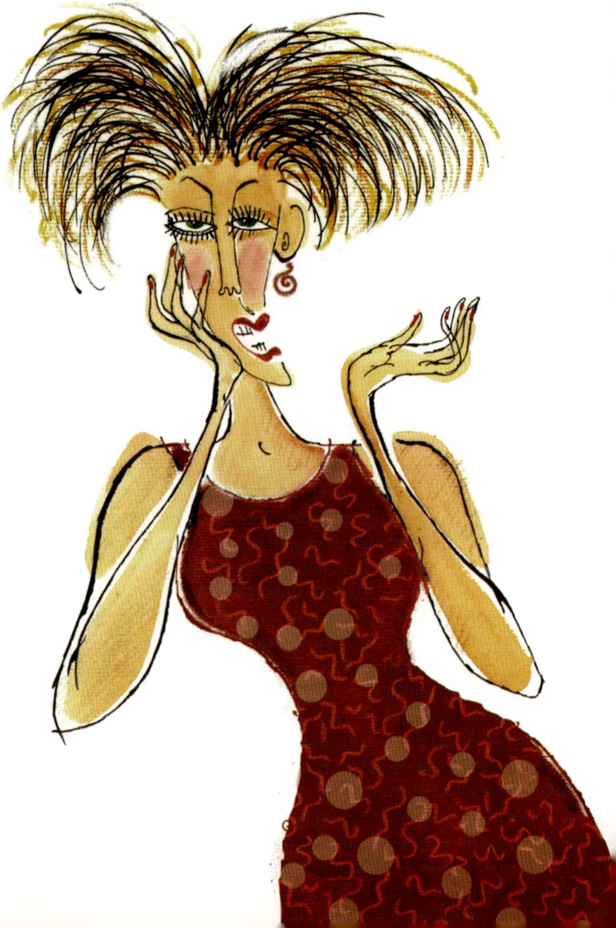

Oh, to be only half as wonderful as my child thought I was when he was small. And only half as stupid as my teenager now thinks I am.

REBECCA RICHARDS

I think it's a mother's duty to embarrass their children.

CHER, B.1946

One knows one's done one's job as a parent properly if one's children reject everything one stands for.

GLENDA JACKSON, B.1936

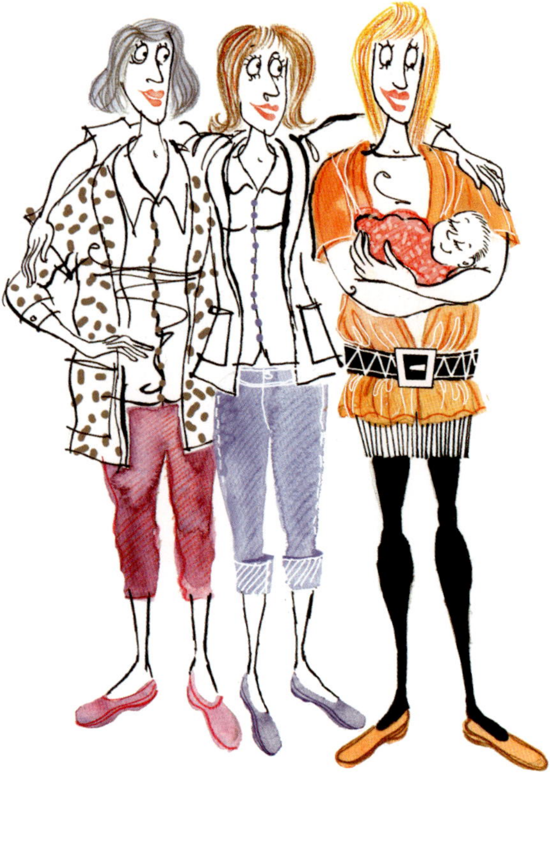

Always another beautiful little horror...

By the time the
youngest children
have learned to keep
the house tidy,
the oldest grandchildren
are on hand to
tear it to pieces.

CHRISTOPHER MORLEY (1890–1957)

A dribble of baby-food on your dress, a splodge of pastry-mix in your hair.... These are the badges awarded to all lovely mothers. Wear yours with pride.

CHRISTINE HARRIS

The Heart of the Family

Like a gentle, enthusiastic and understanding Noah, she has steered her vessel full of strange progeny through the stormy seas of life with great skill, always faced with the possibility of mutiny, always surrounded by the dangerous shoals of overdraft and extravagance, never being sure that her navigation would be approved by the crew....

GERALD DURRELL (1925–1995),
FROM "MY FAMILY AND OTHER ANIMALS"

Mom's Battle Cry quickly and effectively rounds up all her little soldiers from near and far "Time for dinner."

STUART & LINDA MACFARLANE

Thank you for being my mother...

Being a mother
— the hardest job
in the universe,
the toughest job
in the universe,
the most thankless job
in the universe,
but the greatest,
most wonderful job
in the universe.

STUART & LINDA MACFARLANE

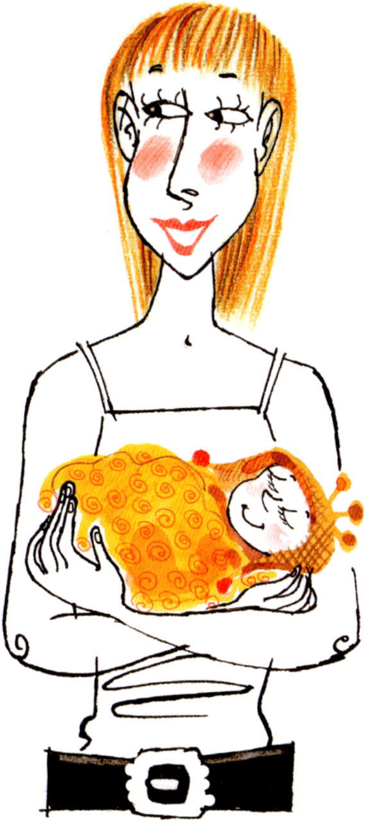

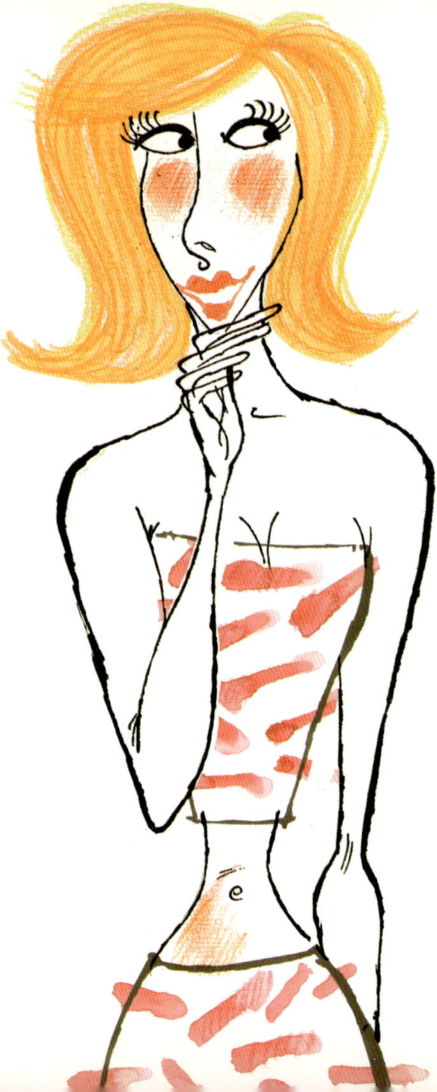

Mother:
Forty percent
intuition,
fifty percent
hard work,
a hundred and ten
percent love.

AMANDA GIBSON

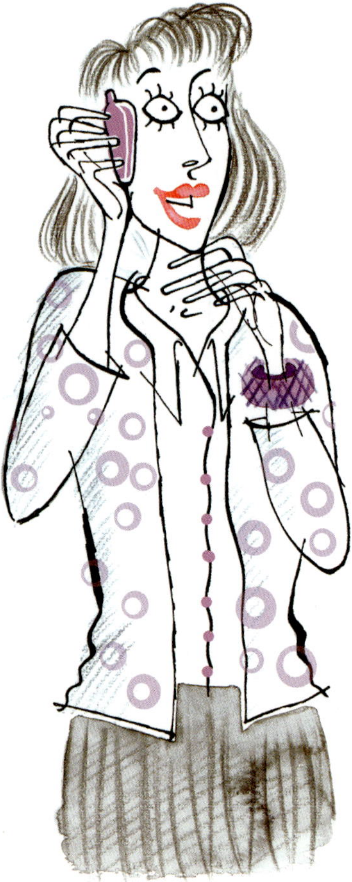

Thank You!

I never knew mothers
minded until I dropped your
rose-covered teapot and
you cried. You said
people were more important
than teapots. But I rather think
that at that moment,
teapots only just came second.
You wait till I'm rich.
I'll buy you a golden teapot.

PAM BROWN, B.1928

HELEN EXLEY

Helen Exley is well-known for her
collections of quotations, with her giftbooks
selling five million copies a year.
Her books are on family, friends and love,
with a strong inspirational addition of
wisdom, personal peace and values books.

"I've created well over a dozen books on
mothers and daughters. Indeed, the whole of
Exley has been firmly based on that central
relationship between mothers and daughters –
growing on to cover the whole family.
As both a mother and daughter, I identify with
Poor Mom – I've laughed and cried as I've put it
to press. And I've felt waves of guilt for not
saying 'thank you' often enough to my own
special mother, for the awful worries I put her
through. So don't you ever forget to say
'thank you' in hundreds of ways, and then to
forgive totally when it's your turn…"

Rowan Barnes-Murphy

Rowan Barnes-Murphy's cartoons are wicked, spiky and frayed at the edges. His fantastically well-observed characters are hugely popular and have been used to advertise a diverse range of products such as cars, clothes and phones, supermarkets, bank accounts and greeting cards.

Other books in this series:
Too Soon for a Mid-Life Crisis
A Woman's Work is Never Done
Girl Talk!
But it's My Turn to Sulk!

For more information contact:
Helen Exley Giftbooks, 16 Chalk Hill, Watford, Herts. WD19 4BG, UK.

Helen Exley giftbooks are all on our website. Have a look… maybe you will find many more intriguing gift ideas!

www.helenexleygiftbooks.com